GIVEN

Conversations with
Florian Tathagata

220
PUBLISHING

First published 2007

ISBN 978-1-905479-03-0

Published by 220 Publishing
PO Box 220, Harrow, HA3 5SW

Printed in India by Thomson Press

Florian Tathagata's website is
www.Tathagata.de

You can contact 220 Publishing at
info@twotwentypublishing.com

TO THE HEART

THE MONASTERY OF SANTUARIO DE CURA, MALLORCA

EMBRACE

The embrace of all the marvellous people who continuously contribute to the creation of these books expands and deepens moment by moment. Thank you to every friend who shares their heart, who is willing to live as love and who is available to be truly met and to meet.

With all love and respect I am resting at the feet of my teacher Isaac Shapiro. You inspire me to live as an embodiment of truth, love and compassion. You remind me of holding the hand of my father, mother, sisters and of all beings the way you hold mine amidst the movements of life. Thank you beyond words.

Thank you to all the following friends who with great attentiveness and precision have read the proofs of this book and made valuable comments:

Dieter Dammert, Kim Somerville, John Stewart, Stephen Thomas, Rick Trask, Ingrid Zimmermann and Julia Zimmermann. The back cover photograph is by my friend Leo Prembuddha Kroonbergs.

Through the past year, friendship with Jim Whiting, my editor and publisher, has gently grown. Thank you for the wonderful editing of the countless recordings that you have transcribed and compiled in this book with love, clarity, inspiration and understanding.

In particular my gratitude belongs to my partner Julia for her support, groundedness and love. On this journey of seven years since we met there has been a natural maturing that has led to our now chairing the meetings and retreats together. Thank you for sharing the fire, passion and love for truth as one heart.

Florian Tathagata

INVITATION

All is given yet nothing is for us. This seeming paradox was a major theme of the meetings and retreats with Florian Tathagata that are the basis of this book. It explores the relevance of these words to daily life by means of edited transcripts of conversations between Florian and participants of retreats and public meetings in various countries.

The conversations throw light on the confusions created by the outward movement of attention from awareness. Awareness is an ever still point and, in the realm of speech, only words coming from this still point can bring the attention back to awareness. From this stillness, mechanisms that habitually play out in us in day-to-day life are uncovered as part of an ever fresh enquiry into what is real and what is not. This enquiry is very grounded, heart-centred and life-enhancing.

Florian frequently speaks of 'the breaking of the heart'. These words can carry some baggage for those of us exposed to sentimental pop songs and romantic novels. In being and speaking with Florian, it has become clear that he is speaking of the heart that is not yet one; the heart of the 'doer'; the heart I protect when reality conflicts with 'me' and 'mine'. The heart that is one is the instrument of pure awareness. The heart that we believe is ours obscures this pure awareness. This is the heart that waits to be broken so that it may awaken to oneness with the universal heart and its embrace of the joy and suffering of all.

In the oneness with all of life to which this book points, everything we think we are dissolves into nothing. This is the essence of being and of love. It is the same with words that speak of our true nature. Only when what we think about them dissolves into nothing can that which they exist to make known be fully realised. I invite you to join me in hearing Florian's words and in being with what they reveal.

Jim Whiting
Editor

SUBJECTS OF CONVERSATIONS

Our home is the unknown.

In the unknown
we are not two.

From the unknown,
Love listens
and from the unknown,
Love speaks.

Where you and I end,
Love begins.

Life is what is given. Life is this moment. Nothing else exists but life creating itself from moment to moment.

But what about the future? This meeting was in the future when it was planned.

The fact that it was planned did not guarantee that it would happen. I also plan to be in India next year, but this is only an idea in mind. I have not the slightest idea if this is going to happen or not. There is an availability in me to be in India next year and life will decide whether it happens, not me. Only when we say 'I have decided' or 'I have to decide' does it seem like I am the decider.

The invitation here is not to make life a personal affair. Let life live you. If you want to live life for yourself, it is stressful and exhausting with some moments of happiness and satisfaction. If thoughts show up, don't make them your thoughts. If feelings show up, don't make them your feelings. Awareness sees things coming and going but takes nothing for itself. That awareness is the truth of who you are.

Is what you are speaking of the same as surrender?

I am speaking of something less than surrender. Surrender needs a surrenderer, and I am talking about being nothing, about not taking. If the experience of now can have you, instead of you surrendering to now, life can take over. The best way I can describe it is being available, because there is no doing involved. It is utmost passivity; unconditional availability to let this moment have you. This moment very gently clears away any sense of me that remains and replaces it by itself. It is most gentle.

You cannot get rid of the sense of I; all attempts to do so keep the sense of I in place. But that which you wanted to overcome is that which sets you free if you are space for it. All we are speaking of is the movement of attention. When attention comes to rest, life brings itself home to us. The sense of you returns into unlimited space; that sense of you merges with its own source instead of trying to overcome itself. The 'old stuff' you think you have to deal with doesn't exist. It is just a collection of stories generated by the movement of attention away from awareness.

The observation of experience causes a distance between you and others. Many spiritual seekers over the years have trained to become the observers of reality.

What has been overlooked is that while there is observing there are still two — an observer observing something external. Can you be here, now, free of the observer?

Awareness is not the observer. The observer is someone who is doing something and this causes a split, a separation. Awareness comes from being, not from doing. Observation is looking from the outside in. You believe that the split this causes protects you — that by observing life it will not be too intense. But it costs you almost all of your energy, and you are never completely available for life so long as this split continues.

It is just a habit; no more than that. Let that habit come to rest.

My stomach is so full of old feelings that I cannot be present with you.

I like to know who you are, but I don't care how you feel. What is of interest to me is if you can be present with your partner when you feel bad. Then I know who you are. What interests me is if you can be the space for your children and not care how you feel. Then I know who you are. What interests me is if you can do what you have to do, however you feel about it. Then I know who you are.

Can you be the space for whatever you experience? Then you can be the space for your partner and your children. Otherwise you are only interested in yourself. You still have a tremendous amount of interest in what you experience in yourself, but this is of no interest to others. I hope you can take this.

I am not interested in saying something that will make you feel good. What is of interest to me is whether you can hear what you know to be the truth and not care how you feel about it.

So who are you? Are you the feelings?

No.

Are you the awareness of the feelings?

Yes.

So who are you?

Awareness.

Yes, you are that which contains everything. Just allow that to touch you. How is that?

Hell and heaven.

Yes, you are the space for hell and heaven. You are prior to hell and you are prior to heaven. So now you know who you are.

When I am in the world and vulnerable, I feel that other people's energies are affecting me. When I was younger I was not aware of it and I never knew why I was feeling the way I did.

You still don't know.

I know when energies are negative and when I am vulnerable to them.

This is something you have heard, but it is not true. It is correct that you feel everyone; this is a capacity that every human being has. It is natural. It is not spiritual and it is nothing special. Mirror neurones in the nervous system have the capacity to reflect the emotional state of each person to each other person. It is nothing you or I do. You cannot turn it off. If I don't want to feel you, I create a separation. This separation is much more painful than feeling any discomfort there is in you. If I try to push you away, the original discomfort stays and the pain of separation is added on top. The pain is doubled. If we can sit together, simply and ordinarily, and very gently allow whatever is in the system to be felt, without trying to solve, without trying to understand or fix or push away, there is an invitation to let it completely be here.

My problem is that there are people I can trust and be like this with, but there are a lot of people around with whom I cannot be so open. I try to avoid these people but it is very exhausting to live like this.

Yes, the pain and exhaustion you are experiencing is not the 'bad energy' of these people, but this subtle movement in you of trying to keep a distance. It is this that makes you feel bad, not the energy of the other people. Have you ever met an angry person and been able to be gentle with him inwardly, not wanting him to be different? Did he calm down?

Yes.

And when you meet an angry person and you react against him, does that person get more angry?

Yes.

The so-called bad energy of other people does not exist in reality. The bad energy is the subtle movement in us. If I try to push you away I am saying I am good and you are not good. If I tell you that you are not good, is that good energy or bad energy?

Bad.

So where does this so-called bad energy come from? It is just a movement in your nervous system. It is not you. Just see that little movement in your system. It has nothing to do with guilt or right or wrong. It is just a little movement you are usually not aware of. If the movement is not seen, we get caught up in funny ideas of right, wrong, guilty, not guilty, bad energy, good energy. We have believed that living like this protected us. But living like this has not protected us, it has just caused a lot of stress and exhaustion.

I feel like a guard has been let down and my energy is moving more freely.

Yes, I feel that. And you feel the circulation of energy in my system too. So can we really talk about 'your' experience and 'my' experience? Or is it that there is an experience that is available for both of us in this moment? It is the biggest waste of time to try to find out where the experience of now comes from. If you go to a therapist because you feel stuck they may have all sorts of interpretations and explanations for you and you will move away from what is real in you. Feeling stuck is just a mechanism of not wanting to be available for the experience of now. That mechanism is the same in everyone. What is bigger or smaller is the number of interpretations placed on top of the mechanism. These interpretations are just a protection of the heart.

What is wrong with protecting one's heart?

Nothing. It causes stress; you feel alone; you feel exhausted and frustrated; you waste your life; you think nothing is as it should be, so you try to change it and you fail; but it is not wrong. It just carries a very big price my friend.

But have you ever had the experience where you had your heart in your hand and someone smashed it?

I know that experience, but I am not talking about being a victim. There is a willingness to let the heart break every moment of my life; a willingness not to protect the heart from pain. Protecting the heart is the way we separate ourselves from others. By allowing it to break, this false sense of separation dissolves.

Whatever happens; if we see something in the world that touches us, be willing to let the heart break, again and again and again and again. Be willing to let the heart break from everything that shows up. Each time the heart breaks, the capacity to love increases. Each time the heart breaks it deepens the capacity to be compassion in an unconditional way. Only a broken heart can love. When one broken heart meets another broken heart, there is only one heart, not two.

What was happening while you were speaking was an apparent choice in some moments whether to go with thoughts or not.

Only when you separate yourself from the thoughts, when you become the observer of the thoughts. Then you have an apparent choice. Only then. It needs the sense of two. In the duality of you and what you are observing in this moment, in this sense of two, the apparent sense of choice shows up also. Let us check this. If there is no observation, can even the idea of choice show up? If you are completely with what is, on a beach with a lovely woman and a beautiful sunset, is there even space for the thought of choice?

I can see that in a situation where there is rest and no wanting there isn't a choice — there's no need for a choice. But situations are not always ideal. In fact most of the time they are not ideal.

They are always ideal. If you say they are not ideal, you already have an image of another 'reality' in your mind and by this you have created the split. In India they say Purnanidam Purnamida — this is perfect, that is perfect. There is nothing that is not ideal to pure awareness.

So if I am sitting lost in thought, that is ideal?

Yes. Because you have no other choice. In this moment, anything you see about yourself is a created object like anything else in awareness. The moment you see this, you do not have to worry about it. The worry is generated by the idea that it could be different. If thinking is happening and there is an image of a being that is not thinking, the thoughts go back and forth between what is happening and the untrue image. You do not have the choice not to think.

What about conscious choice?

Conscious choice does not need a chooser. It is a matter of what we are available for. If there is a lot of pain in us, or if there is still a lot of restlessness in us because of stress stored in the nervous system, we very quickly can become available for thinking. I can be available for resting, because I have seen this is the only thing that makes sense; it is enjoyable and it brings about a clarity. What could be called conscious choice comes from this, not from me. But this body for quite a lot of its life was available for thinking. Instead of being available for the beloved moment to kiss me, I was available for thinking. So it is just a matter of availability. The availability for thinking is a protection of the heart, because we do not want to feel the pain, sadness, anger, fear and so on that is there. We do not want to feel life in its fullness, just the nice bits, so life sends us thinking as protection.

In seeing that going on isn't there an opening up to the dropping of that protection?

Yes. There can be an opening up when first you are completely gentle with your own hardness. You become gentle with the hardness that your system has habitually generated. You don't do the hardness. It just plays out. The belief that hardness will lead to freedom can be quite deep in some of us.

Do I have a choice about what I am available for?

It is not about having a choice. It is about gently being available as awareness. If you are available as awareness, if you live as awareness, then awareness will take over as the fruit of letting go of the idea that you are the doer. This is not a choice; it is a recognition of what you are and then living as that. It is letting life choose you. Many are called, but few are willing to let life choose them.

Awareness is the creator.

Trying to change anything
is manipulation of creation
and it does not work.

In humbly responding to
awareness, and what it shows,
a new world is created.

But it has nothing to do with us
or what we think we want.

This is freedom.

If you are involved in self-improvement, you are working on something that is not your concern. The way you are is not your problem. When you take it as yours, your whole system shifts into 'I need to solve a problem'.

There is nothing to solve; there is only something to see. When your whole system shifts into 'me' mode you lose almost everything of value. There is no brightness and no fun, and no real contact is possible.

The moment you start to be real — start to be yourself — you meet yourself. When you meet yourself, everyone feels met. To meet yourself is to rest in the experience of now. There is no-one there trying to meet; there is no-one trying to be available. It is just availability. You cannot do it. It is a natural consequence when you give up the doing.

Be what you truly love instead of talking about what you would like to be.

Yesterday I found myself making a problem when there wasn't one.

This is a common way of returning to the framework of 'me'. If nothing is wrong, we very quickly create a little problem so that there is still something to solve — still something that keeps me in the picture. There are a lot of problem addicts about, because most people have a problem with being uncontracted. They need some friction to make them feel they are still alive.

Then I realised there was nothing to do.

Yes, that's right, but beware. If that is heard from the framework of 'me' then the 'me' takes those words to protect itself from being fully available. This is the Advaita trap: 'Nothing is real'. There are things in life that are challenging, but these are not the problem. The problem is that we usually approach these challenges from a place in ourselves that I call contraction. So when there is something that needs to be solved — and in daily life there are plenty of things that need attention — we are usually not aware of just how contracted we are. And when we approach a situation from that contraction we are not seeing much. We are just reacting to what a limited and narrow focus of attention can perceive.

Yes, difficult situations in life do bring on a contraction in me.

It's the other way round. It is not that the difficult situations bring on a contraction. The contraction is the source of the problem; not seeing the whole is the source of the problem. If a decision is made from a place of contraction we will soon see that some aspects have been overlooked; then we have a problem. Instead, rest as awareness.

So, I rest as awareness and see what happens?

No.

Wait for a solution to be given.

No. You have added something to what I said. If you want to see what happens or if you wait for a solution to come, you become the observer and there is a subtle doing involved. Just rest as awareness, with nothing added. Being the observer is not resting as awareness. Only when you are nothing can you rest as awareness.

I am not clear about the difference between a contraction and a feeling.

A contraction in the physical system is deeper than a feeling. It is in the cells — a contraction in the tissues that we frequently jump over. When we jump over a contraction, an emotion is generated. Then the mind tries to solve the feeling and gets caught up in abstractions. The mind says if you do this or do that you will get rid of the contraction, and it is just adding another layer. The more you think, the more you contract. But at root it is just contraction in the body against which there is an emotional reaction. Contraction, emotional reaction, mental processing: these are the layers.

You cannot solve a contraction at the emotional or mental levels. The invitation is to see this process operating and to be with the contraction without trying to solve it.

From the perspective where we say 'not now' to an experience, life looks like a threat, but it is the not wanting the moment that is the only threat. This movement of not wanting the moment is usually missed, so the threat is usually perceived to be life.

What I find in myself is a shield protecting my heart, a shield full of concepts and ideas about finding a perfect relationship.

I know what you speak about. It was the biggest dream of my life to have a perfect relationship. I was ready to do everything a human being can do to have one. And I did. And the more I did the more I messed it up. I was so stubborn that even after many relationships that I screwed up by having a good intention, they still ended up the same way – separation. "You don't give me what I want; I can't give you what you want", so we separated.

The shield is the idea of a perfect relationship, which is a very naïve and immature dream. Can you gently let that idea of the perfect relationship be here without believing in it? If you believe in it, it will keep you searching for the rest of your life. There is no such thing as a 'perfect relationship'.

There is also a belief in me that I need a partner in order to be complete.

The truth is exactly the opposite. The partner is

not to make you complete. If the partner is living what nature wants from her — living fully as a woman — you will not be made complete. You will be reduced to your own essential nature, the male principle of beingness.

A partner brings not a completion but a reduction. She reduces to what she truly is, acknowledging her natural existence, and the man reduces to what he truly is. It is not about being a better man or a better woman. Through this reduction to our essential natures, wholeness can come into existence; the false is stripped away.

In India, they say that resting beingness (Shiva) cannot live without the dynamic principle (Shakti) because it would be just lost in the void. The dynamic principle cannot live without the resting beingness, otherwise it would end up as a never-stopping pulsation — complete chaos. We have not understood this. Most spirituality seeks to transcend this natural limitation.

Between man and woman there are impossibilities, and you will never make them possible. That is why all my concepts and your concepts about a perfect relationship failed. The concepts fail because they cannot bring peace. Peace comes when we acknowledge that there are impossibilities between a man and a woman that we can never solve. There are things we want from the other that they cannot give and there are things they want from us that we cannot give. We could call it the imperfection within the perfection. This is truly perfect. When we can gently acknowledge this, we become very compassionate with our impossibilities, and from there we can meet our partner with the same compassion.

So when your partner does not understand you, be grateful that she does not understand you. For then she gives you the opportunity of giving up your need to be understood. This giving up of your need – rather than being 'completed' by having it met – brings peace immediately.

I cannot accept it when my partner puts pressure on me – I behave like a three-year-old who doesn't want to be told what to do.

So you blame her when she puts pressure on you? Instead you can play a little game of thanking her for the pressure and then find the gift that it contains for you. Where you blame the other, if you give up the blame you will find the greatest gift. It is there you will find the diamond; not in wanting the other to change. It's a nice little play. You can try it with any relationship – business partner, children, parents, brothers and sisters. Inwardly thank them for being exactly as they are, for it shows up what needs to be shown up in you.

Relationships help you to see where you are not honest with yourself and others and where you protect your heart by keeping a sense of separation alive with a bunch of relationship concepts. So thank her that she does this, because she must be interested in your freedom. If she did not serve you in this way, I would doubt the love.

An intimate relationship is a space in which all thoughts, feelings and sensations – including the darkest places in ourselves – show up. These darkest places cannot show without such a relationship. Awareness penetrates every obstacle when we meet each other in the space of awareness rather than from a personal standpoint. A close relationship shows you just how enlightened you really are.

It is not about solving problems or getting rid of pain. It is about living with dignity and with a sense of full responsibility for your personality, patterns and pain; blaming no-one – not even yourself.

Life to me is not a big supermarket where I can use anything and everything to get rid of my pain. It is a rare opportunity in gentle humility to experience what destiny wants and to carry this in love for truth. Life is not about getting what we want, but gently living what is meant to be.

The circumstances of life
are never the problem.
Every problem you ever had
was nothing but a contraction
you tried to get away from.

Can you be the space
for an unsolved issue,
without making a choice?

Then awareness can explore.
The situation can reveal
its own solution to you,
without you getting involved.

GIVEN

As a man I feel I have to be clear. It causes a lot of pain in me and others when I am not clear.

How do you know this?

It's the feedback I get. Also the churning of thoughts in my mind.

Do you believe the feedback? Or can you just listen to it and see what may be true and what is not true. The pain is not what the others feel; it is the way we take it personally.

I feel I am responsible for the pain of my partner.

Yes, that is the pain we are causing for ourselves. That we still believe we are responsible for how our partner feels.

That's a strong belief, yes.

You believe that if you were different, if you were more loving, if you were the ultimate husband and the most gentle lover, your partner would not feel any pain any more. So that is the pain you feel — not the pain of your partner, but the pain of wanting to be different. Not wanting to feel the pain of your partner without taking it personally, and wanting to do something about the pain, is a protection of the heart from breaking.

The intention I see behind it ...

Wait. Give yourself a little more time, because your system is very quick. It is so quick that you do not give yourself the space to feel what wants to be felt. The mind is quick. The heart is slower. If we are willing to let the heart break, we give ourselves a moment of time. Do not try to understand or analyse. Don't involve the mind. There is a tendency in most of us to very quickly make everything abstract. This tendency is an aloof perspective. It may convince us that we are making a valid attempt to understand what is going on; but we are not able to feel what is going on. I doubt that your partner has ever had the chance to fully feel you. I know this tendency very well from when my partner and I first met. That same thing was in me.

Yes, I see that I try to make my partner happy.

That is the sunny part of it. The dark part is trying to change her, using everything you have ever heard in your life, and believing that you can only be happy when she changes. So our concern about our partner's pain is not really altruistic. We love to believe we do it only for them, but this is just an image we have of ourselves.

There is something that can be very irritating for our partners and for other people. When a feeling presents itself in us, the mind is very quick to analyse that feeling and turn it into a sort of knowledge or wisdom, and we can delude ourselves that we are above it, that we have dealt with it.

Can you let your heart melt instead of being a wise man? Just allow yourself to be present and allow yourself to experience and feel whatever is here, without any attempt to understand or manipulate it. Don't make yourself feel. Just feel what wants to be felt.

I am not interested in what you know or in what you have found out about life, but I love to meet you in your joy and I love to meet you in your pain — everything that is real in you. There we can meet each other as love.

A decision will show up
when it shows up,
not one second before
and not one second after.
I am not involved in this.
If I try to get involved
because I think I can
speed up or improve
the process, I believe that
God or reality may make
a mistake without me.

GIVEN

I like to get close to other people and am often in-sensitive to the fact that others do not always want this. I don't feel their barriers.

Because this wanting to be close is for you.

Yes.

It requires quite a mature sensitivity to feel what is appropriate in each moment. This maturity is possible when you can simultaneously hold yourself and the other person in awareness. Then there is not a subject and an object — someone who wants something from another person — but a play of awareness; a play between two objects in aware-ness. Then you live as a huge embrace of yourself and everyone else. Absolutely anything you can be aware of, including yourself as an individual, is an object in awareness, and in truth there is no subject. As this non-subjective and non-objective awareness, you live as a huge embrace of yourself and everyone else.

In this huge embrace it is natural to feel the need of the moment. You can only jump over the need of the moment when you split yourself and believe yourself to be the subject and everything else to be an object that belongs to you. This perspective comes from early childhood. As a little baby, we lie in our bed and cannot move from it. All we can do is cry or scream whenever we need something. The brain of the baby recognises that when it cries, the mother comes to meet its needs. When it smiles it gets a kiss. The baby feels itself to be the centre of the universe with tremendous power to get others to move according to its wants. Much New Age thinking comes from this. It carries the belief 'I am God' and 'I can make all things possible'. Much 'creative visualisation' is just wilfulness based on 'what I want for my life' and requires a subtle violence to ourselves and others to create what is visualised. It is a very immature way of seeing things. It is thinking that the universe belongs to me.

Ultimately we come to see that it is not that the universe belongs to me, but that in all humility I belong to the universe; it is not that life belongs to me, but in all humility I belong to life.

The only reality is awareness – the infinite and eternal space that is here, now, and holds all objects in its huge embrace. We belong to this.

The utmost wakeful passivity of awareness is very relaxing. We do not have to carry the burden of creation on our shoulders and we can let life do the job. You are relieved of the belief that you are an individual who has powers. All is given, yet nothing belongs to us. If we can live this paradox, there is infinite peace. We just let life show us how life is.

This wakeful passivity does not mean that no action takes place. It just means that attention rests while the body is fully active. Then life can move freely in you. You are the space for that life, the non-activity in which activity happens. While I am speaking, nothing is moving in me. I do not even know who is speaking; there is no-one there, just awareness.

The invitation is not to love everything, because you cannot do this. If you live as gentleness there is no doing. It is a way that life can meet you. It is not an activity, not a discipline, or something you should do. Love is nothing you can do. You can only be it without trying. People who try to be loving are mostly very violent to themselves. Every time they think they are not loving, they beat themselves up in the name of love and they think that if they beat themselves up enough they will become a loving person.

GIVEN

My experience of life so far is one of a strong pendulum swinging wildly from one side to the other.

You are speaking of something that is old, a loop that you no longer need to believe in. Have a look to see if you really believe in this loop, this vicious circle.

While I am sitting here, it makes no sense.

No it does not, and you do not need to change the loop. There is a recognition of it and you know exactly what the loop looks like and how you feel when you are being drawn into it. You know how the sound of your voice is affected by the loop and how your body moves or sits when you believe in it. The loop that you have identified as who you are is a problem causer, and you do not need to live with these problems. You can just notice the loop and ask yourself 'Do I really believe in this?'. Then you will get an answer, and more than likely the answer will be no. And in this moment the loop comes to an end, softly. Going into it has just been a habit. Not going into it is a new habit. The new habit is to invite awareness; sensitivity. It is a new road; not the problem road.

This loop has in fact been a quite immature way for you of trying to meet another.

Instead of just resting within and meeting in a straightforward way, you have generated a little drama or story because you believed this would get others to give you attention. Finally you would get acknowledgement and understanding for this, but this old habit does not really work. It prevents real meeting; a real meeting between you and the other as awareness. With your partner you have sought to get attention by using this habit, but it has prevented you really meeting him.

In society, women are still often considered as powerless – that the power is still in the hands of men. The opposite is the truth. The female has such power on the one hand to bring about a problem or conflict or on the other of providing awareness and caring. Most of the women I have met do not know about this. In some way they believe they are victims of men, and that if men change they are going to be happy.

I can see that now. I did not understand it before.

You just see it in a very clear and gentle way. It does not have to play out again and again. It can come to rest. It will cause a tremendous shift in the way you can meet your partner and others.

What is of value is to see the pain that the habit has caused – the pain of not meeting. Every time you went down that road you added another layer of pain on top of the pain. So just don't follow the habit anymore. Follow the new habit of not following it.

Then you can begin anew. It is a confused perspective to try to take apart the loop bit by bit. If you do not believe in the loop at all you cannot believe any part of it. You solve the whole thing at once. You see the loop, you know where it will end, and you gently do not follow it anymore.

If you want to rest in life,
there will be no rest.

Instead, allow life to rest in you.

You are rest.
Allow everything in life
to rest in you.

This is true rest – living as rest
rather than looking for life
to give you rest.

Sometimes when I look at you I can really sense the joy you speak of.

Yes, but it is not your joy or my joy. It is just joy that is available for everyone.

The moment we take it for ourselves the sweetest joy turns into bitterness, because by taking it we limit it. We take its vastness and try to fit it in our own framework to make it ours, but that joy is not the same joy anymore. It becomes very small, and we have to be very protective so that no-one takes away that little piece of the cake.

So every time you want to hold on to something, you are losing it?

Yes. The moment you take it for yourself you lose it. It's gone. It's a paradox: when we don't take it, it's always available, always given. But it's not for us. And who cares that it is not for us? If it is there and it can flow through the system, why do I need to own it? This is a very mature way of living, or of letting life live you.

Before you can hold on to something, you must first take it. So do not take it in the first place, because holding on and protecting it takes such an incredible amount of life energy. You are left with a little crumb instead of being available for the whole cake.

It is difficult to realise the price I pay, because it is the normal way I live life.

But you are realising it right now. Is it difficult?

No, but it seems like I want to hold on to the pain and my patterns.

It may seem like that, yes. But it is not true that you want to hold on to pain.

First of all, it is not your pain. Second, they are not your patterns. The mistake is to think they are yours. Whatever is repeating is not for you. I am not neglecting the fact that sometimes there is pain; I would be a fool if I did. But it is not for me and it is not for you. Why should you hold on to something that is not yours? In truth you cannot hold on to something that is not yours. Holding on needs 'me' and 'mine'. Without 'me' and 'mine' holding on has no substance. The idea of holding on cannot survive without 'me'.

Have you tried to let go? You cannot. No-one has ever succeeded in letting go. Letting go is not for you. Letting go is the end of someone trying to let go; so do not try to let go. It will strengthen the whole game. Don't try to not think; it will strengthen the thinking. Don't try to transcend your patterns; it will strengthen the patterns. The biggest pattern of all patterns is trying to get rid of patterns.

What should I do then?

Nothing. Simply be available for this moment to kiss you. When your partner comes home, you are available for him to kiss you. Maybe he will, maybe he won't; but you are available. Then the kiss is really sweet, because it is free of 'me'. Let whatever is here now kiss you. Just receive life without doing. Just receive what is given.

We are so busy living life, we have largely forgotten what it is to simply receive life and let life live us; to be unconditionally available for this moment to have us and to recognise that every moment is the beloved, whatever it contains. This moment is it. In this moment, the beloved kisses you. This moment is God.

Now I can see the beauty of resting in the present moment, but I know that pain and sadness will come back.

More than likely things will show up. The only thing that can turn everything into another problem that 'you have' is thinking that it is your pain that shows up. Then the life that you see here and now as impersonal very quickly becomes a personal affair again. Then this impersonal freedom that you are now experiencing is replaced by you needing to find a way to deal with life. Unhappiness needs you. Without you, you cannot be unhappy. Without 'my experience' and 'my pain' unhappiness cannot survive.

The worst that can happen is that when a tendency or sensation shows up, you pick it up and believe it is yours. From there, life certainly moves in another direction; it moves in the direction of having a personal drama: a tragedy with some moments of comedy. Joy is when this sense of 'me' — this self-centred activity — comes to an end. By recognising it is not you, it falls back into nothing-ness by itself.

Yes, I see that.

Now, let this understanding have you. If you think you have understood, you have taken it for yourself. But if you live as an embodiment of understanding, every moment of your life is an expression of that understanding. And every moment when you see you have not been in integrity with what you are, just allow that seeing to touch the heart so that the understanding may deepen.

There is a tree of pain and a tree of sweetness. If you sow seeds of pain, more pain will grow. If you want the sweetness, sow the seeds of sweetness. The seeds of pain are personal; the seeds of sweetness are impersonal, so sow the seeds of sweetness. To live as this understanding is to live nakedly, without a sense of self-security. We cannot have the sense of 'being someone' and at the same time live as truth. When I saw this I went to my teacher and said to him 'I don't like this; I feel so naked and so helpless. All my sense of self is gone'. In his simple and loving way, he smiled and said 'Make this your home'.

At the moment I think everything is about me. I want to be the one sitting here with you talking about me and my story. I want to solve something and I don't even know what I want to solve!

Thank you for being honest. There is a huge price to pay for this thinking. We can live like that — around six billion people do — but what is the cost?

The cost is that there is no peace.

That's right. There is no peace, and no joy, no meeting, and no connection. The biggest cost is that as long as we live from that perspective we are never available. Our parents cannot meet us, our friends cannot meet us, our partners cannot meet us. When you are focused on yourself, no-one can meet you. The invitation of our meetings — and it is quite a rare invitation in the world — is to be here for this meeting instead of being here for yourself.

A child thinks that his parents are there for him, so it is a mature perspective to be here for others. You do not need to do anything; I am not talking about 'doing good'. You are just here so that everyone and everything can meet you. You are not here for yourself; you are here for life.

There is a melting away of tension.

And this melting away of tension is not for you: it is not that you find peace, but that the seeking for it stops. You become the space in which everyone finds peace, and if you stop looking for peace from others the gift others bring you is peace.

I noticed at the end of this morning's meeting that for years there has been a condition in me saying I have to grow up and be independent. Yet fighting my feeling of dependence and being resistant to it fails every time. The more I want to be independent the more I end up being dependent and not at peace.

Of course. You become what you fight against. Everything you include brings peace. Peace is beyond dependency and independence. You live as peace so that everything can be free in you; everything can come home to you. This is living as freedom from dependency, but there is no-one there who is independent. The independent 'me' is dependent on others to be independent from.

The person you
believe yourself to be
never really existed.

It is an illusion
created by the movement
of attention from
awareness to experience.

GIVEN

I experience a lot of opposition in my personal and professional life.

Whenever you encounter opposition in life, it shows you have taken a position. No position, no opposition. So this can be a tremendous opportunity for you to see where you keep the world outside of you — where you are separating yourself by maintaining positions or points of view.

Identifying a position is very easy. First it shows up as a contraction. Second, it is usually accompanied by some kind of consideration of self-image or ways of doing things that we hold onto. These are positions and we contract around them.

This is painful for me to hear.

Yes, to look at oneself is always painful because more than likely we will see things that are quite ugly and that we tend to project outward. The moment we see something about the way we are being that is not very nice we tend to throw it at others.

And vice versa.

Yes, but we have no control over other people. They may, they may not.

You say that thoughts and feelings don't matter.

Thoughts and feelings are not a problem. They are unavoidable. For me, thoughts are present sometimes, but thought in mind is like having a radio on in the background without giving attention to it. To be the space for thoughts and feelings is to allow everything to show up in consciousness without picking it up and without jumping over. One of the traps to avoid is jumping over thoughts or feelings; the subtle pretending that they are not there. This causes problems because the thoughts and feelings are not included in consciousness; they are pushed aside.

So can you be the space for thinking and feeling and all the sensations, noticing them very sensitively and just allowing them to be in the system? Another way of saying this is that we are not having a feeling but the feeling is having us; we are not having a thought but the thought is having us; we are not having sensations in the body but the sensations in the body are having us. This perspective avoids the huge trap of jumping over. If we want to get rid of thoughts, feelings and sensations we are keeping life outside of us; we are not integrated, and this causes problems.

So we have to go through it all.

No. It goes through you, because you are the space. You don't have to go through anything. Life moves, not you. You are not in life, but life is in you. And what is life? Life is all the thoughts, feelings and cellular sensations in the physical system that are in consciousness in this moment. Your body is an experience in consciousness. Your body is contained in you; not the other way round. I also am in you. I am an experience to you. I am already contained in you, so it doesn't make sense to keep me out. You are aware of me; you are aware of yourself; you are aware of all experience that is happening now. Trying to get rid of any of it is just a funny idea, but most of the people on a spiritual path are, in my experience, trying to do just that.

Gently be willing to let
the heart break.
It is not about being a victim;
nor any romantic notions.

It is about gently allowing
ourselves to be touched by
whatever is at the core of being.
It is about allowing the heart
to be naked.

When the heart is naked,
doership dissolves
into pure awareness
and pure response.

I am able to rest at complete peace but there are still things I need to learn.

Let's explore the idea of learning. We have funny ideas like being in a process of learning or having some things we need to learn. What is the idea behind these? What is the promise of learning?

Change.

Yes, change. Once we have learned something, what is the promise? That things will be better, or that we are not going to repeat the same mistake. This is the idea behind learning.

My experience of life is that when it has been really challenging I have learnt something from it.

Let's check if you really have learned something or if it just seems like you have. Did you really learn something or did you stop learning about it? What you are looking for is to be in peace with something. The promise is that when we have learned enough we are going to be at peace.

Yes, but learning from it brought me greater peace than I had before.

True? Or has the situation turned into peace? If something has turned into peace it is not bothering you anymore.

I don't think I follow.

The particular situation that has been challenging, just allow it to be in you now. Just be the space for the whole situation – every aspect, the people who have been involved, and the system you call you. How is it if you are just the space for this challenging situation? Invite it into you, without learning from it, without figuring something out.

My mind is still trying to figure out an answer.

OK, this is part of the challenge. The challenge is continuing because you haven't found an answer. Let this unsolved question be in you. Feel it in your body. Let your body respond to it.

My body and my mind are still trying to escape from it because it is not comfortable.

Let this movement of trying to escape come a little closer. Just feel the running; just allow the whole situation to have you. And see if you can find that place in you where you can be grateful that this situation has been part of your life.

I am not there yet.

OK, have another look. Don't push it; don't force it. Just look to see if you can find a place in you where there can be anything to be grateful for in the situation. The tiniest little bit is enough; where you can say thank you.

I cannot find anything.

Can you see that the situation is bringing something into consciousness that you have not been aware of so far?

Yes.

Is it a gift to become aware of something that you have not been aware of so far?

I think I have been aware of it but it is knocking at my door saying this really needs to be dealt with. I don't know how to deal with it.

You can say thank you for knocking on my door because you are showing me something that I do not feel secure with yet. Now by knocking so clearly on my door, I see that I still keep you outside. Can you be grateful for this?

Yes (hesitantly).

That is all that is needed. Saying thanks for being shown that there are ways in which you still protect your heart. This is the gift. How is it if you see it from that perspective? What do you feel in your body?

Loads of fear.

Now you are meeting those places in you that already have been operating all the time, but you kept them at a distance. When they showed up, you said 'leave me alone'. Let the fear come a little closer. Whatever you call fear is just a sensation; nothing else. It is a contraction in your physical system; there is no need to name it fear. Where do you feel the contraction?

Pretty much in every muscle in the body.

It is some tension that has been operating all your life. Maybe you haven't been aware of it, that's all. You have adapted to it, but have not been at peace with it. Now the stress energy is going down, through the feet.

As soon as that happens it starts coming back up again and I start thinking 'but Oh my God what am I going to do?'.

There is nothing to do. Just notice the sensations in your system and any change in the flow of energy.

It feels just not as panicky anymore, but I know that the panic is going to come back.

It may or may not. It's not about what comes back. It's about the way you are with it. We cannot avoid experience. Our nervous system is organised around the belief that when we have tried hard enough or when we have learned all we need to know, then we may no longer have certain experiences. But this is not the way it works. We cannot control life by learning. It's about the way we are with whatever shows up, not learning a lesson so that it won't show up again.

The habit of becoming tense and heavy is so deeply in the cells that the body starts to do it by itself. If you see this — and you will be astonished how often the body does it — you can give the cells new information. What used to be a habit to walk or sit in one way can be changed to a more useful habit in which the body feels more easy and light. It is a shift of presence, just letting the energy flow differently in the body.

Instead of walking, let yourself be walked. It is the same energy as the energy of breathing. If you think you breathe, check it out. After thirty seconds you will see who's breathing. It is not you breathing, but life breathing through you. The belief that we are breathing comes from the same thinking that believes we are doing anything. But it is not like this. Live life without the burden of 'my life'.

I have a question about forgetting. Awareness includes everything — the good, the bad, the feeling, the not feeling — everything. But I often forget this. When I do forget, is it enough to include the forgetting as well?

Yes. Awareness includes the forgetting.

As simple as that?

Yes.

So it's OK to forget?

Absolutely. The more you can be at peace with forgetting, the more you will remember. The more you try to remember, the more you forget. The more you try to be conscious, the more self-absorbed you are. The more you relax, the more you are awareness.

In this moment all I can feel is now, but a habit is arising to hold on to this state of presence.

Yes, but this state is not for you. In truth it is not a state, but when we take being in the now for ourselves we turn it into a personal experience and automatically create the fear of losing it again. The reality is that the moment we turn it into an experience or a state we lose it. It is given, but it is not for you and it is not for me. Knowing this, we transcend peace. We are free of the need to be in peace; and this is true freedom. So long as we hold on to a particular experience, we are not free. As soon as we take peace for ourselves, it becomes another prison.

This habit of taking things for ourselves turns everything into a personal affair, and then we lead a life that is 'my life' – my unsolved problems, my drama, my childhood, my spiritual development, my enlightenment, my resting. But all this is not for you. It is for no-one.

In that easiness that you are, everything is welcome to show up, without you taking it and without you doing something with it. It is just welcomed. We can laugh in the midst of uncomfortable feelings because they are not even ours. Then, out of love, we are available to be kissed by whatever shows up. Everything can meet us. It is not that we meet it, but we are available to be met – by everything. Life can only function like this; it cannot be different. Human history has proved that it cannot be different, for we have tried and failed. The other way is not functioning.

While the full range of experience is happening here, from gratitude to the dark side of the range of feelings, it is not you. The invitation from heart to heart is not to pick up one single experience, not to make it yours. Just allow it to touch every single place in the system that it wants to touch, without you doing anything with it. You are that utmost simplicity in which the multiplicity of life can move freely.

Yes, I can feel a strength that isn't impressed by any of these things that are going on.

It's the strength of availability; the strength of resting; the strength of not doing. It is the biggest power in the universe. We can call it beingness, we can call it love, we can call it availability. But it is definitely not doing anything; it just is.

Not even the picking up is ours; otherwise everything would be not for us except the picking up. The picking up is just a habitual movement that is flying around the universe. Absolutely nothing is for you or for me; so there is nothing to be afraid of.

I am alternating between this freedom and the contraction that occurs when I cease to experience it.

That alternation is also not for you. There is a noticing of it and then your system has taken it, labelled it and turned the alternation into a personal experience.

Yes.

So now there is someone there who experiences alternation between freedom and contraction – an experiencer and an experience, an observer and an object being observed. But this experiencer, this observer, has no real existence. We are touching the deepest layers of the sense of separation, of the sense of two. It is a reflex in your system. It is not for you.

Are you constantly arguing with reality because you think you know better? This is the way most people live most of the time. When we see through the belief, we can be grateful. Perhaps for the first time in our lives we can be generously and gently grateful: 'Thank you for this moment'. Then instead of life being an expression of subtle complaining, covered with some nice spiritual icing sugar so that it is not quite so painful for you and others, life becomes an expression of thank you.

I feel stuck and I don't know why.

Get a sense of how you meet this stuckness that you feel. Are you soft with it or are you hard with it? Are you trying to push it away?

Get a sense of who you are with that experience, so that you start exploring beingness, not the experience. You explore who you are in the midst of that experience. This is not what you normally do.

No, and it is a bit uncomfortable.

Yes, because you now meet yourself. To meet our experience is no big deal, but to recognise who we are amidst experience throws up sides in us we do not like to see.

It shows us the way we are with ourselves and the way we are with others. Can you meet the discomfort you feel with gentleness; without wanting to change it; without wanting it to get better?

This is very unfamiliar to me.

Yes it is quite naked. Shields of protection become

transparent. We can see how ugly we can be from time to time. When you are gentle with yourself, that ugliness turns into compassion.

So gently invite everything that you do not want to see about yourself. It is not about hardness; it is not about judging; it is just about reality, the reality you have been ignoring. There has never been any ignorance except your own. Truth is not interested in comfort or familiarity; truth is only interested in reality. But to be interested in reality has nothing to do with being hard on yourself. It is about being naked and vulnerable; about dropping the protection of the heart.

How can I be naked and vulnerable and still function in everyday life?

Very simple. Just don't try to figure out what is going on. The mind likes to work in a linear way, but reality is not like that. Reality is full of paradoxes that the mind cannot solve. So do not try to figure out what is going on in your experience and don't try to figure out what is going on in you. Then you constantly live nakedly. You always live as an availability for reality to meet you. Then reality shows you how it actually is.

It's a habit, the way we have been brought up. In our culture, we are taught to concentrate, know what we want to get in life, go for it. That is one part. Then most of us are carrying a tremendous amount of stress energy in the nervous system. And what is stress energy? It is a contraction. The stress energy in the nervous system is causing constant contractions; we have become used to them.

The nervous system generates a contraction, then we focus on the contraction and we build up a relationship – a contraction and a person trying to solve it. Trillions of cells are communicating with each other and functioning in a particular way that gives you the feeling of being separate from the whole. So the individual you believe you are is just trillions of cells organised around stress. But actually there is nothing there.

Having an expectation is a stress isn't it?

Yes. When you want something, the system tightens up and the thinking thinks if you get it you are going to get rid of the contraction.

So if you have a need, how do you deal with it? Do you just let it go? How do you avoid having expectations?

I can't avoid having expectations because they are part of the functioning of the nervous system. But the expectations are not who I am, so the question is not what can I do but how am I with them. How do I meet the contractions? Can I be soft with them? Whenever I did something with a contraction it was always related to getting rid of it and this placed another layer of contraction on top of the original contraction. This never worked. When I do not add anything to a contraction there is an invitation for the contraction to soften.

When I speak about not moving, I am not talking about physical movement. I am speaking of allowing attention to come fully to rest, so that the otherwise constant movement of attention — what do I think? — what do I feel? — what do I want? — can come to rest.

You cannot stop the movement of attention, but in not moving with it it may come to rest. We only move with it because we habitually believe its false promise; the promise that we will get what we want, or get rid of what we don't want, if we follow it. But it always ends up in disappointment.

So the invitation is to directly meet what is. This can become a new habit. I do not invite you to follow me; I invite you to join me in not moving.

I always feel I have to be doing something or being someone. It is hard to be nothing.

Not for me. I am happy to be nobody. It is much more relaxing. My body is still able to do its job. The moment I show up as someone, things do not move so nicely anymore. It is for the benefit of all of us if there is less of me. And you too are much more relaxed now. Are you doing anything? Are you being anybody – someone specific?

No.

Nothing to do, nothing to be, nothing to know. Nothing has been changed, but you are different. You are softer now with whatever is, much softer. And in that softness everything softens.

The more the nervous system is under stress, the more distorted our perception. We even see things that are not there; the senses function differently. The world is experienced as a threat. The stress in the nervous system creates distorted perception and the distorted perception creates further stress. It is a loop. When we are soft with what is, stress energy is discharged, a new loop is created and the world is seen as a friendlier place.

Whenever you are attracted
to something or someone
it is always the love in you
that you feel, not something
outside of you.

It is not your love
or their love.
It is just love.

Many on the spiritual path have picked up the habit of observing themselves. They saw that there was something more to life, so they started to observe what was going on in their relationship with the world. That became a habit that is now counter-productive. Many so-called 'spiritual' people cannot meet others without an observer in between.

The invitation is to be without that habit, so that you neither look outward nor inward, but passively see what shows up. Noticing what shows up is enquiry. Enquiry does not need an active observer. It takes place in awareness.

Earlier this year I went to India for three weeks and felt very good. There were no thoughts.

If I give you a litre of wine and you drink it all, you will have no thoughts. Or you can smoke a joint and you will have no thoughts. All it means is that you have no thoughts, nothing more.

But it felt very good.

Yes, of course, but if you want a good feeling you don't have to go to India. I understand what you mean, but the interpretation that has followed the experience may be misleading you. Having an empty mind is fantastic, but it doesn't mean anything. It was just an empty mind, and now it isn't empty anymore. The empty mind has been an experience. A full mind is also an experience. Both are experiences, and all experiences come and go.

But this experience continued for six months longer and I was hoping it would last.

Yes, and it didn't. That's it. It did not last because no experience lasts. The nature of experience is change. The whole world is an experience. What the world is to us is an experience in us. When we believe that we want to have another experience, we try to get rid of the experience we are having or we try to change it.

Can you allow the experience you are having right now to be here? Can you feel the experience in your body? You can only experience life through the body. Most people who go to India to find a guru or start seeking enlightenment do so because they think that after enlightenment they will never have to experience pain anymore. But this is not true.

(Laughing) If I had known this I would never have started to search!

You have just overlooked one simple little fact. There is no way to avoid life. Even enlightenment will not save you from being fully alive.

You cannot be at peace with life if you are busy dreaming of something better.

Life is giving itself moment to moment and you can only receive what is given when you are totally passive.

So long as you are busy inwardly or outwardly, you cannot receive.

GIVEN

One moment I was sitting here very still and peaceful and then suddenly I became angry about something.

Every day things show up in experience that we do not like. You are feeling good as you come home and when you get in you find that your partner is in a bad mood. One minute life is blissful and we feel completely free, the next moment something is triggered in us and the freedom is gone. This is no problem.

The question is not what am I experiencing, but how am I meeting what is being experienced. What makes the difference is the way we can meet whatever shows up in us. In our culture, the point of life has become how to make our experiences better. We live in such liberal times that virtually any experience it is possible to have can be had, but people are not happy with this. Have you ever been made truly happy by a good experience?

No.

No, and the reason is simple. An experience has a beginning and an end. When we cling to our experience we lose our innocence. The moment the good experience ends, we have a memory of the experience and we want it again. Then we are caught up in the wheel of having experiences. This is part of our culture. There is an experience and what we add to it is a tendency to get caught up. You were able to see the anger coming up, so you were not caught up in it. There was no playing out of the aggression.

When I became angry I decided not to go there.

You were not the one who became angry, nor the one who decided not to get sucked in to the anger. Both of these were part of what you experienced. The normal thinking is that I am having an emotional reaction and I am suppressing it, working it out, integrating it, or whatever. But have a look. Did you do the anger? Or did it just show up?

It just showed up.

Then there was another movement that avoided the anger. Did you do that?

I had the feeling that I did.

Now have another look. Did you really do it or did it also just show up?

The movement happened and I took it over.

There was a movement of not wanting to have the aggression. We could call it resistance – a thought along the lines of: 'I am here and everything is peaceful around me; I do not want anger right now'. Who did the not wanting to have the anger? Did you do it or did it also just show up?

It showed up.

Yes. How does it feel if you just allow the experience of now to come into you without thinking and believing that you are doing it? Nothing has to change: you don't have to change; the experience doesn't have to change. It is just a matter of the way you are with that experience. Either you think you are doing it or you know it to be given and there is a gentle invitation in you for the experience of now to be completely here – even the anger, whatever. Can you allow the anger to come home without playing out? And instead of having the experience, allow the experience to have you. How is it, when you are the space to let this moment have you instead of trying to deal with the experience.

I feel alive. But it also feels fragile. It is a state I cannot maintain.

Yes it is most fragile, because we are not used to it. We are not familiar with letting life have us. In our culture we think we have to deal with life: it seems like life is something outside of us and we have to deal with this big thing called life. But this is not true. So allow that fragility — which is also an experience — to have you. Don't do anything with it, don't try to maintain it. Invite it into you. How is it if you allow this fragility, this gentleness, this fineness, to be in you? It's relaxing isn't it? And it touches the heart.

Yes, very much.

Instead of trying to find a job that you love, let the job that you have find the love in you. If people worked like this, the world would look very different. Work would become a living prayer. Whatever job you have, if you think that you are the doer, it will end up in stress and dissatisfaction. If you want change, you will soon see that what you change to does not give you what you want. But if you just allow the job to have you, see if it is the same.

One of the biggest confusions of the esoteric movement is that people think they have to find their destiny. There is no such thing as a personal destiny. No-one has a destiny, because life is not for us. We are for life; and when we are seeking we are not for life.

Haven't the most beautiful times in your life been when you had no plans? Once we have a destiny or a goal, the beauty of the moment is lost. It is not that life does not offer goals, but taking the goals and making them yours causes confusion. We can only be ourselves with empty hands; because anything we take covers who we are.

Living what we love is
understood by the mind as
'how can I get what I want?'
Or 'how can I
have what I love?'

The real question is
'how can I live as love?'

We are then in service to
that love instead of being
driven by our likes and
dislikes.

I have a contraction like a tight belt around my stomach.

Usually when we wake up in the morning, a contraction takes place very soon after, and we move through the day with it until we end up exhausted in the evening. Allow that sensation in the body, that habitual contraction, to be as it is.

(Pause).

It is much less now.

Yes, and it is less in the others in the room also, so we cannot even say that it was your contraction. It does not belong to anyone. It is not personal; ninety-five per cent of a contraction, of tension, is the belief that it is yours. If you take away the pressure of believing it to be a personal experience, if you take away the belief that it is yours, what is left?

Not much.

Not much — so it is good to see that. Now, whatever is left, allow that residue to completely have you. Don't deal with it; don't solve it; don't try to figure out what it is; don't close your eyes; don't look at it – just let it have you.

I feel the contraction is getting stronger again now.

Then you are doing something. If you do something with it, it gets stronger. What you are doing is observing it, and that observation is causing a little distance. I invite you neither to observe it nor to focus on it. Just rest as that awareness that is aware of the sensation. Just be that awareness, without focusing anywhere.

How is that?

Much softer.

Yes. Part of the contraction is the focusing on it; this puts your energy into it. You want to get rid of it by observing it, but it is making it worse. If you observe your thoughts, you get more thoughts. If you stop observing your thoughts, they are gone.

It is an endless loop. You observe your thoughts, you generate more of them and you can easily become a therapy case for the rest of your life. It is a self-generating mechanism. My invitation is to softly meet all those places in you that are still a little bit tight; to meet every little sense of un-happiness, every emotion you do not like to feel – don't jump over. Allow that sense of unhappiness that is still there to be fully in awareness. It is not personal. There is nothing wrong about you. The unhappiness just wants to come home into awareness. It is not about trying to change it or finding out where it comes from. It is about welcoming it as the love that you are.

Can you be light amidst pain and darkness? Or do you believe that pain has to be suffered while you look for a solution to it? Instead of trying to find a solution, allow the attention to drop from the mind into the sensations of the body. Whatever the sensations are let them make love with you. When we feel discomfort we habitually try to figure out where it comes from and how we can remove it. Can you be with it without wanting it to be different?

When you can be love with your own sensations — however they are — you can be love with other people — however they are. Can you see that when you distance yourself from your own experience, you distance yourself from others? All separation begins within. It is a shutting down of the awareness that you are. It is not a matter of sharing pain nor denying the pain, but gently being light in the midst of pain.

Can I decide to let go of my ignorance?

No. You let wisdom decide. You just give yourself completely to wisdom. Then every decision comes from that wisdom, not from you. When wisdom decides, it brings more of itself; it generates more wisdom. If a sense of me decides, it generates more of a sense of me. An apple seed generates an apple tree. Everything generates only more of itself; it cannot do anything different.

So gently be aware of where you start from, because you recognise this will generate more of itself. Then you never touch pain again. Pain may touch you — this is part of human life — but the moment you touch pain, pain becomes suffering.

When you start from wisdom, the Prodigal Son returns to his father. Wisdom and you become one. You can recognise this only because you have spent some time away from home. You do not need to worry about the time you have spent from home. The father — wisdom — calls you home. Giving yourself to him is enough. Be carried by wisdom.

The more I honour,
what I know is true,
the more I live
what I love the most.

I often act against my inner guidance.

If you believe in inner guidance, which is basically a psychological process or feeling, and then action is in another direction, you will have a big conflict because you split yourself into a good part and a bad part: a good I and a bad I, a guiding I and an I that misguides you. If we believe in two 'I's – a higher I and a lower I – then confusion is caused because the truth is that there are not two. This is the cause of the warfare in you; because these two ideas are fighting with each other, but neither idea belongs to you. The substance of the dialogue between them is thinking.

In not feeling connected with life we habitually and easily connect with thinking. We divide ourselves into parts that communicate with each other. These illusory parts try to meet because we are not available for life to meet us. Artificial relationships are built up with thinking, feelings and the body as a substitute for a pure and innocent meeting of life. Recognising this dialogue in you between a higher I and a lower I, you become aware you are not that dialogue. You are the space and the peace in which this game can happen without you becoming involved.

Addiction is still part of my life. Once it was addiction to smoking, at other times to women, and now it could be to spiritual teachers.

You say you have been addicted to smoking or to women, but this is not the reality. What you have been addicted to is a certain inner feeling that is generated by these objects. It is a chemical process in yourself that you are addicted to. It has nothing really to do with cigarettes or women, or anything else. These just generate a particular biochemical cocktail in your system which makes you believe you need more of it.

This biochemical cocktail is experienced as an emotional state that feels like 'who I think I am'. An alcoholic needs a particular amount of alcohol in the blood to feel normal. If the alcohol level drops below this, he feels he needs something in order to feel normal again. It is the same with the cocktail of chemicals in our blood.

Nothing has access to an agitated nervous system unless we can meet it. The will has no access to it, reason has no access to it, the emotions have no access to it. Only silence within can bring it to rest. What people experience during a silent retreat is excess energy discharging from the nervous system. The system starts to rest. Sense how the nervous system is functioning in this moment. Let the attention drop into the body and sense from inside how the nervous system is functioning right now.

There's a subtle activity.

Yes, it is subtle. That's why we usually miss it. We miss it because we do not give ourselves the time to sensitively meet the sensation on a cellular level. When we jump over this subtle movement the senses turn outward and we start looking for cigarettes, alcohol, women and so on.

This coming to rest: does it mean to not act out the longing or to see that the longing is a lie?

Both. The first thing is to see that every thought and every feeling that shows up contains the promise that if you pick it up it will lead to peace. If you don't believe this promise any more, what happens then?

Strong sensations.

Yes, in that moment we can meet the actual sensations. When we pick up the false promise we are artificially quietening the sensations. So in not believing the promise, first of all the sensations can seem to become stronger. But they are not actually stronger; they just seem that way because we are not covering them any more. They can show themselves as they are.

The invitation is, with utmost gentleness on your part, to let these sensations come to you; to let them be in you. If you are hard with them, they do become stronger. Then you think you cannot bear them any more and you believe you have to do something or take something to relieve the pressure. The intensity is not their nature; it is generated by a movement in us away from experiencing them – so the energy again turns outwards. The natural movement is when we just rest and allow the sensations to come to us. When they come home, they come to rest.

The beautiful thing about reality is that it knows nothing about guilt. This moment is fresh and innocent. If we have missed a chance to be soft, we are so lucky because in this moment we have another chance. We can still be beating ourselves up now for being hard yesterday or half an hour ago. So then we were hard and now we are hard too. We continue to try to be soft by being hard. We beat ourselves up in the belief that if we keep being hard then one day we will learn to be soft.

The softness I speak of is meeting our own sensations with utmost gentleness; gently resting amidst this moment. Softness is not something you can do and it is not a feeling. It is a way of being, and that softness penetrates our feelings and our thinking. This is the fruit of softness. Working on yourself doesn't function − it cannot function.

How can children be given the understanding to remember themselves when they have forgotten? I was travelling on the bus recently and there were two parents who did not seem to know what to do with their child who was crying all the time.

This question touches my heart, because if we raised our children with that understanding, this world would be completely different. This world would be an expression of peace rather than an expression of trying to create peace.

There are so many things in the world that want to be met. They don't want to be changed. The normal reaction to the situation you have just described is to think there is something wrong. We may interfere in some way. But we do not know what the child has to go through and we do not know what the parents have to go through.

The other possibility is to completely meet that situation. Let the heart break by what is appearing in front of the eyes. That unconditional compassion with the child, with the parents, with the whole situation, with every other person on the bus who doesn't know what to do, holds all this in consciousness, in the unprotected heart. To live as that can bring a tremendous awareness to the situation. That seed of awareness is available to everyone in the situation from the moment we rest in awareness and allow the situation to be completely in us. In that moment, everything that is there — the thoughts of the parents, the feelings of the child, the helplessness of the other bus passengers — is penetrated by that awareness. People can always feel this.

It is not that you are bringing awareness to the world; to believe that would be an ego trip. You just sit there and rest as awareness without wanting or needing others to know. You offer that awareness to the situation. You hold the awareness in which you appear and also the others. It is not that you are aware and the others are ignorant. It has nothing to do with you. You don't get spiritual with them, you don't get psychological with them, you just quietly invite them as they are into you. If we believe the awareness is ours personally, we start telling people what to do so that they can be as enlightened as we are.

In the end we do not look
anywhere anymore.

The seeking ends and seeing
happens without a seer.

And what is seen?
Beauty; the movement of life
as it is.

Do not fight worry. When worry comes home to softness it turns into a beautifully innocent insecurity, because you really don't know what the outcome will be. The more you let things be, the deeper is the love.

We cannot be love if we are not naked. As long as we are holding on to something, or we have a sense of self-security to protect, we cannot be love. Love is always completely naked, not knowing what will happen.

When you are helping someone, are you directing your energy from you to them?

No, because this is not help. It is the avoidance of helping. The other day someone came to me who was working with drug addicts and alcoholics — young people in an institution. He was exhausted. We had a conversation and he suddenly realised for himself that he saw these young people as addicts, and saw himself as a helper for those addicts. The way he was seeing them was strengthening their tendency to drink or take drugs.

So the next time he met them as a group he did not have the label 'addicts' in his mind. He did not have the image of 'helper' anymore; the game of helper and addict came to rest. Suddenly they could meet. A lot of weight fell from his shoulders; there was easiness and lightness. Therapists and helpers easily generate co-dependency.

I was at the local train station at home a few years ago waiting for my partner so that I could drive her home. The station was in a fairly rough area. There were some young men drinking and fighting about ten metres away. One of them came over to me. He was quite tall and carrying a can of beer.

I had no idea what was going to happen. We were looking at each other and I asked him where he was from. He told me he had just come out of prison and that he lived on a farm. He told me that all he had learned were fighting and drinking. He spoke for about ten minutes and as he spoke he became softer and softer; he started to cry. He said it had been the first time in his life that someone had listened to him and that he had felt he had been seen. There was no doing involved; no image of helper on my part: just a natural response. I had no sense there was anything wrong with him.

Is there a pattern in the people who come to these meetings that we come to get help from you for enlightenment? Do we have to do it by ourselves?

You can neither come to me for enlightenment, nor can you do it by yourself. Enlightenment is not a personal affair. So long as you come to me to become an enlightened person, you will be disappointed. The invitation of our meetings is to receive; but it is not that you get something from me, because I cannot give you anything. We share a love for truth. We speak together and meet each other so that life can awaken us to itself.